Table of Contents

B Demure

The Ultimate TikTok Quizbook

A History of TikTok

1. Who created TikTok?

    a. Mark Zuckerberg ☐

    b. Kevin Systrom ☐

    c. Zhang Yiming ☐

    d. Jack Dorsey ☐

2. Which year was TikTok first launched?

    a. 2016 ☐

    b. 2017 ☐

    c. 2018 ☐

    d. 2019 ☐

3. What was the original name of TikTok?

    a. Musical.ly ☐

    b. Dubsmash ☐

    c. Triller ☐

    d. Video.ly ☐

4. TikTok is Primarily known for which type of content?

    a. Short Videos ☐

    b. Live Streaming ☐

    c. Podcasts ☐

    d. Music Videos ☐

5. What type of video was the first uploaded to TikTok by the co-founder?

    a. Dancing ☐

    b. Lip-Synch ☐

    c. Music ☐

    d. Life Hack ☐

6. What was the original maximum length of a TikTok video?

    a. 5 seconds ☐

    b. 7 seconds ☐

    c. 15 seconds ☐

    d. 30 seconds ☐

7. TikTok's logo features which of these colors?

    a. Blue ☐

    b. Green ☐

    c. Red ☐

    d. Yellow ☐

8. What is the page called that suggests videos for you on TikTok?

    a. Trending page ☐

    b. For You page ☐

    c. Discovery page ☐

    d. Exploring page ☐

9. Which company develops TikTok?

    a. ByteDance ☐

    b. X Corp ☐

    c. Shanlist ☐

    d. Meta ☐

10. What country was TikTok developed in?

    a. China ☐

    b. United States ☐

    c. Great Britain ☐

    d. India ☐

ANSWERS

Section one: History of TikTok

1. C - Zhang Yiming
2. A - 2016
3. A - Musical.ly
4. A - Short Videos
5. B - United States
6. C - 15 seconds
7. C - Red
8. B - For You page
9. A - ByteDance
10. A - China

/10

SECTION TWO

Stars on TikTok

1. What Men in Black star is the most followed actor on TikTok?

   ....

2 Can you smell.... Who the most followed wrestler on TikTok is?

   ....

3 What K-pop band is the most followed on TikTok?

....

4 Which UK chef is the most followed Brit on TikTok?

....

5 What European Soccer club is the most followed on TikTok?

....

6 Who is the most followed Mexican on TikTok?

....

7 Which 'Kardashian' is the most followed on TikTok?

....

8 Despite no longer holding the record as the most followed TikTok account – which American star still ranks #1 in most liked videos?

....

9 James Stephen Donaldson has over 83 million followers. He is most famed for Youtube videos with big money giveaways and has more recently transitioned to TikTok – what is he more commonly known as?

....

10 One of Britains most followed TikTokers is just 18 years old. He has 25 pets and his videos range from animals to food and life hacks – who is he?

....

ANSWERS

Section Two: Stars on TikTok

1. Will Smith

2. The Rock

3. BTS

4. Gordon Ramsay

5. Paris Saint-Germain

6. Kimberly Loaiza

7. Kylie Jenner

8. Charli d'amelio

9. Mr Beast

10. Kyle Thomas

/10

SECTION THREE

TIKTOK EARLY YEARS

1. In 2017 TikTok increased its maximum video length to how long?

    a. 30 seconds ☐

    b. 60 seconds ☐

    c. 90 seconds ☐

    d. 120 seconds ☐

2. What was the name of the challenge that saw users appear to be frozen in place?

    a. Frozen in time challenge ☐

    b. Freeze challenge ☐

    c. Mannequin Challenge ☐

    d. The Statue Challenge ☐

3. How many languages is TikTok available in worldwide?

    a. 10 ☐

    b. 20 ☐

    c. 30 ☐

    d. 40 ☐

4. What is the Chinese equivalent of TikTok?

    a. Meituan ☐

    b. Wechat ☐

    c. Douyin ☐

    d. Tencent ☐

5. What is the majority bracket of ages that use TikTok?

    a. 13-17 ☐

    b. 18-24 ☐

    c. 25-34 ☐

    d. 35-44 ☐

6. In 2018 Lil Nas X released which song? – TikTok played a major part in it becoming the longest number-one song in US chart history

    a. Industry Baby ☐

    b. Montero ☐

    c. That's what I want ☐

    d. Old Town Road ☐

7. In the first half of 2018 TikTok was downloaded over 100 million times from which location?

    a. Google Play ☐

    b. The App Store ☐

    c. Amazon ☐

    d. GetJar ☐

8. Within a year of TikTok which milestone did it surpass in terms of number of views per day?

   a. 1 million ☐
   b. 5 million ☐
   c. 10 million ☐
   d. 1 billion ☐

9. What word became popular on TikTok to describe those of an older generation?

   a. Bloomer ☐
   b. Boomer ☐
   c. Gloomer ☐
   d. Doomer ☐

10. And what name is given to the current generation? Widely used on TikTok

   a. Generation A ☐
   b. Generation D ☐
   c. Generation X ☐
   d. Generation Z ☐

ANSWERS

Section three: TikTok early years

1. B – 60 seconds

2. C – Mannequin Challenge

3. D - 40

4. C - Douyin

5. B – 18-24

6. D – Old Town Road

7. B – The App Store

8. A – 1 Million

9. B – Boomer

10. D – Generation Z

/10

TikTok Trend Videos

Who created the following TikTok Trend Videos?
Initials provided to provide a little help

1. The Renegade Dance	JH
2. Magic Ride	ZK
3. Christmas Sisters Party	JC
4. "M to the B"	BP
5. Time Warp Scan	BE
6. Mouth Drawings	FB
7. SugarCrash Lipsync	NL
8. CM on Bro	KL
9. Frog in Closet	NS
10. Sail	JK

ANSWERS

Section four: TikTok Trends

1. Jalaiah Harmon
2. Zach King
3. James Charles
4. Bella Poarch
5. Billie Eilish
6. Frank Bielak
7. Nick Luciano
8. Khaby Lame
9. Nadir Sailov
10. Jordi Koalitic

/10

SECTION FIVE

TikTok Stats

1. What is the most popular content category on TikTok? It has amassed 535 billion hashtag views.

    a. Dance ☐

    b. Pranks ☐

    c. Fitness ☐

    d. Entertainment ☐

2. How many times a day does the average user open TikTok?

    a. 12 ☐

    b. 19 ☐

    c. 25 ☐

    d. 30 ☐

3. How many years did it take TikTok to pass 1 billion users? It took Facebook and Instagram 8-15 years.

    a. 1 year ☐

    b. 2 years ☐

    c. 3 years ☐

    d. 5 years ☐

4. How long did it take the developers to create the original version of TikTok?

    a. 30 days ☐

    b. 200 days ☐

    c. 300 days ☐

    d. 365 days ☐

5. What Percentage of TikTok users have bought a product after watching a live TikTok?
    a. 10% ☐
    b. 25% ☐
    c. 50% ☐
    d. 75% ☐

6. How long does the average TikTok session last?
    a. 10 minutes ☐
    b. 20 minutes ☐
    c. 25 minutes ☐
    d. 30 minutes ☐

7. What percentage of the worlds 5 billion internet users have used TikTok?
    a. 10% ☐
    b. 30% ☐
    c. 40% ☐
    d. 60% ☐

8. How many TikTok videos are watched on an average internet minute?
    a. 50 million ☐
    b. 75 million ☐
    c. 100 million ☐
    d. 160 million ☐

9. How much is it reported that TikTok will pay influencers to join the site and make content?

    a. $500 ☐

    b. $1,000 ☐

    c. $10,000 ☐

    d. $25,000 ☐

10. TikToks Creator Fund pays 2-4 cents for how many views?

    a. 100 ☐

    b. 500 ☐

    c. 1000 ☐

    d. 5000 ☐

ANSWERS

Section five: TikTok Stats

1. D – Entertainment
2. B – 19 times
3. C – 3 years
4. B – 200 days
5. C – 50%
6. A – 10 minutes
7. B – 30%
8. D – 160 million
9. A - $500
10. C - 1000

/10

SECTION SIX

THE HYPE HOUSE

Can you name the 10 members of the Hype House that was released in January 2022? Initials provided to assist

1. CH	
2. ND	
3. TP	
4. LM	
5. MH	
6. AW	
7. JW	
8. KA	
9. VH	
10. JD	

ANSWERS

Section six: The Hype House

1. Chase Hudson
2. Nikita Dragun
3. Thomas Petrou
4. Larri Merritt
5. Mia Hayward
6. Alex Warren
7. Jack Wright
8. Kouvr Annon
9. Vinnie Hacker
10. Jacob Day

/10

TikTok 2019

1. What is the name of the dance that involves pretending to drive a car whilst dancing to "lalala" by Y2K

   a. The lalala dance ☐

   b. The Oh No dance ☐

   c. The Oh Na Na Na dance ☐

   d. The Ooh Lah Lah dance ☐

2. What is the tag #furrypotato used to post pictures of?

    a. Disgusting Food ☐

    b. Cute Animals ☐

    c. Poor Fashion ☐

    d. Dad Dances ☐

3. Breaking a Guiness world record in 2019 – a video with over 8 million likes saw Abheesh P Dominic successfully smash 122 of what item with one hand in one minute?

    a. Coconuts ☐

    b. Watermelons ☐

    c. Windows ☐

    d. Iphones ☐

4. What did @jefo Dance for that 6 million people viewed and many others followed?

    a. Dinner ☐

    b. Doughnut ☐

    c. Chocolate ☐

    d. McDonalds ☐

5. Charli D'Amelio posted her first video in 2019
   – how old was she?
   a. 14 ☐
   b. 15 ☐
   c. 16 ☐
   d. 17 ☐

6. And in what state was she born?
   a. Connecticut ☐
   b. Massachusetts ☐
   c. Pennsylvania ☐
   d. Delaware ☐

7. First performed in October 2019 - what is the
   first move of 'Renegade'?
   a. Clap ☐
   b. Dab ☐
   c. Woah ☐
   d. Figure of 8 ☐

8. Which Adele song was used on a video that features a lone Gummy Bear start to sing as the camera pans to hundreds of gummy bears appearing to sing back as though at a live concert?

    a. Someone Like You ☐

    b. Hello ☐

    c. Rolling in the deep ☐

    d. Easy on Me ☐

9. A level up challenge for pets saw dogs jumping over which items as more were added to go higher for each level?

    a. Baked Bean Cans ☐

    b. Cans of Coke ☐

    c. Lego ☐

    d. Toilet Paper ☐

10. In 2019 TikTok added a live feature to allow live streaming for followers to watch. How many followers do you need to be able to go live?

    a. 100 ☐

    b. 500 ☐

    c. 1000 ☐

    d. 5000 ☐

ANSWERS

Section Seven: TikTok 2019

1. C – Oh Na Na Na Dance
2. B – Cute Animals
3. A – Coconuts
4. B – Doughnut
5. B – 15
6. A – Connecticut
7. C – Woah
8. A – Someone like you
9. D – Toilet Paper
10. C - 1000

/10

TikTok 2020

1. Released in August 2020 whose 'M to the B' lip-sync video was the first to reach 1 billion views?

    a. Zach King ☐

    b. Bella Poarch ☐

    c. Jamie32bish ☐

    d. Nyadollie ☐

2. What was the most popular TikTok trend of 2020?

   a. The Twilight Comeback ☐

   b. Ratatouille ☐

   c. The Renegade Dance Challenge ☐

   d. Patience Challenge ☐

3. In 2020 the song Rasputin became a popular meme – who recorded the original song?

   a. Boney M ☐

   b. M People ☐

   c. The Police ☐

   d. The Shadows ☐

4. What is the name of the TikTok dance that involves moving your arms in circular motion and pointing to the ground?

   a. You Can Do dance ☐

   b. Say So Dance ☐

   c. No Way Dance ☐

   d. For you Dance ☐

5. Khaby Lame posted his first video in March 2020 – what African country was he born in?

    a. Nigeria ☐

    b. Malawi ☐

    c. Cameroon ☐

    d. Senegal ☐

6. Also, in March of 2020 who released a single called "Addison Rae"?

    a. Kanye West ☐

    b. Drake ☐

    c. Cardi B ☐

    d. The Kid Laroi ☐

7. TikTok was banned from which country in 2020? At this point it was the largest marketplace

    a. China ☐

    b. Japan ☐

    c. India ☐

    d. Indonesia ☐

8. In 2020 which e-commerce platform added TikTok to its portfolio allowing online merchants to sell directly on TikTok?

    a. Shopify ☐

    b. Amazon ☐

    c. eBay ☐

    d. Opencart ☐

9. What happens in the "flip the switch" challenge?

    a. Two people fighting ☐

    b. Two people switch clothes and positions with the lights off ☐

    c. Two people dancing in the dark with torches ☐

    d. Turning the light off in public places leaving everyone in darkness ☐

10. What song by Drake was used in this popular video?

    a. One Dance ☐

    b. Gods Plan ☐

    c. Rich Flex ☐

    d. Nonstop ☐

ANSWERS

Section Eight: TikTok 2020

1. B – Bella Poarch
2. C – The Renegade Dance Challenge
3. A – Boney M
4. B – Say So Dance
5. D – Senegal
6. D – The Kid Laroi
7. C – India
8. A – Shopify
9. B – Two people switch clothes and positions with light off
10. D – Nonstop

/10

SECTION NINE

TIKTOK 2021

1. In 2021 TikTok increased the maximum length of video to how long?

    a. 2 minutes ☐

    b. 3 minutes ☐

    c. 4 minutes ☐

    d. 5 minutes ☐

2. What is the name of the TikTok challenge where users show their before and after make-up transformations?

    a. Make up challenge ☐

    b. The beauty challenge ☐

    c. Glow up challenge ☐

    d. Beast to beauty challenge ☐

3. Nathan Evans went viral in 2021 for cover versions in which type of music?

    a. Sea Shanty ☐

    b. Jazz ☐

    c. Country ☐

    d. Bluegrass ☐

4. By 2021 TikTok had surpassed a milestone of how may downloads?

    a. 100 million ☐

    b. 500 million ☐

    c. 1 billion ☐

    d. 3 billion ☐

5. What TikTok hashtag led to a marked increase in sales of literature to young people?

     a. #BookTok ☐

     b. #BooksRus ☐

     c. #BooksFORYOU ☐

     d. #Yourbook ☐

6. More females use TikTok than males. What was the approximate percentage of female users at the end of 2021?

     a. 55% ☐

     b. 65% ☐

     c. 70% ☐

     d. 75% ☐

7. In October 2021 TikTok launched a feature to allow users to tip creators directly. How many followers did you need as a creator to activate the 'tip' function?

     a. 10,000 ☐

     b. 50,000 ☐

     c. 100,000 ☐

     d. 1 million ☐

8. What sports organization is the most popular sports brand with 15 million followers?

    a. NFL ☐

    b. NBA ☐

    c. FIFA ☐

    d. ICC ☐

9. @arshoni10 made what product vanish in front of astonished people?

    a. Milkshake ☐

    b. His shoes ☐

    c. A cigarette ☐

    d. Coffee ☐

10. What line was used popularly in 2021 when someone succeeded at a task – such as delivery driver hiding a package or someone showing off impressive weight loss

    a. I understood the assignment ☐

    b. Mission Accomplished ☐

    c. I conquered ☐

    d. You said. I did ☐

ANSWERS

Section Nine: TikTok 2021

1. B – 3 minutes
2. C – The Glow Up Challenge
3. A – Sea Shanty
4. D – 3 Billion
5. A – BookTok
6. A – 55%
7. C – 100,000
8. B – NBA
9. D – Coffee
10. A – I understood the assignment

TIKTOK 2022/23

1. 10-minute maximum videos were introduced in what month of 2022?

    a. February ☐

    b. April ☐

    c. June ☐

    d. August ☐

2. As of July 2023 who is the most followed TikTok user?

    a. @khaby.lame ☐

    b. @charlidamelio ☐

    c. @bellapoarch ☐

    d. @addisonre ☐

3. The most viewed TikTok to date is Zach Kings illusion of which character?

    a. Peter Pan ☐

    b. Spiderman ☐

    c. Harry Potter ☐

    d. Superman ☐

4. Which country has the most TikTok users?

    a. China ☐

    b. United States ☐

    c. India ☐

    d. Brazil ☐

5. What is the name of the most followed animal on TikTok with 19 million followers?

    a. Jiffpom ☐

    b. Cutepug ☐

    c. Littlemoo ☐

    d. Missmouse ☐

6. Nyadollie is famous for what types of videos?

    a. Dancing ☐

    b. Beauty ☐

    c. Lip-sync ☐

    d. Life Hacks ☐

7. Which DJ performed a live stream in October 2022 that broke all TikTok live stream records amassing 638,400 unique viewers?

    a. Calvin Harris ☐

    b. Tiesto ☐

    c. Eric Prydz ☐

    d. David Guetta ☐

8. What is the most followed sports broadcaster on TikTok with over 36 million followers?

    a. Sky Sports ☐

    b. BT Sport ☐

    c. ESPN ☐

    d. Fox Sports ☐

9. The Hype House first aired in January 2022 - what platform was it released on?

    a. Amazon ☐

    b. Netflix ☐

    c. Youtube ☐

    d. Disney Plus ☐

10. What song by Nicky Youre & dizzy was subject to 8.9 million videos being made?

    a. Sunroof ☐

    b. Bad Habit ☐

    c. Vegas ☐

    d. Thousand Miles ☐

ANSWERS

Section Ten: TikTok 2022/23

1. A – February
2. A – Khaby Lame
3. C – Harry Potter
4. B – United States
5. A – Jiffpom
6. B - Beauty
7. D – David Guetta
8. C – ESPN
9. B – Netflix
10. A - Sunroof

/10

SECTION ELEVEN

Famous Surnames

Write the surname to the famous TikToker. First Initial of surname provided

1. Dixie	D
2. Loren	G
3. Addison	R
4. Zoe	L
5. Jaden	H
6. Nessa	B
7. Jackson	F
8. Madi	M
9. Peyton	C
10. Chase	H

ANSWERS

Section Eleven: Famous Surnames

1. D'Amelio
2. Gray
3. Rae
4. LaVern
5. Hossler
6. Barrett
7. Felt
8. Monroe
9. Coffee
10. Hudson

/10

TikTok Songs

Can you name some of the most popular Artists from TikTok song names provided?

1. Cannibal	
2. Yummy	
3. Blinding Lights	
4. Say So	
5. Savage	
6. Boys	
7. Breezeblocks	
8. Shawty in luv	
9. The Box	
10. Uno	

ANSWERS

Section Twelve: TikTok Songs

1. Ke$ha
2. Justin Bieber
3. The Weeknd
4. Doja Cat
5. Megan Thee Stallion
6. Lizzo
7. Alt-J
8. Playboi Carti
9. Roddy Rich
10. Ambjaay

/10

Score Totals

Section one	History	/10
Section two	Stars	/10
Section three	Early Years	/10
Section four	Trend Videos	/10
Section five	Stats	/10
Section six	Hype House	/10
Section seven	TikTok 2019	/10
Section eight	TikTok 2020	/10
Section nine	TikTok 2021	/10
Section ten	TikTok 2022/23	/10
Section eleven	Surnames	/10
Section twelve	Songs	/10
Total		/120

That completes the quiz and with a total of 120 points available – where do you stand?

101-120 Global Superstar

76-100 National Icon

51-75 TikTok Trender

31-50 Room for Improvement

16-30 You have no fans

0-15 Switch to Twitch

Hopefully you have enjoyed this little quiz book and it has been a challenge but your knowledge has extended and been rewarded. Now it's time to challenge your friends.

Take away multiple choice options for the easier questions.

All information is accurate at time of writing July 2023

Future additions and enhancements will come in due course